# The Adventure Begins

_____

_____

# My Cruise Trip Daily Agenda

| PAGE | DAY | ACTIVITIES | PLACE | DATE |
|------|-----|-----------|-------|------|
|      |     |           |       |      |
|      |     |           |       |      |
|      |     |           |       |      |
|      |     |           |       |      |
|      |     |           |       |      |
|      |     |           |       |      |
|      |     |           |       |      |
|      |     |           |       |      |
|      |     |           |       |      |
|      |     |           |       |      |
|      |     |           |       |      |
|      |     |           |       |      |
|      |     |           |       |      |
|      |     |           |       |      |
|      |     |           |       |      |
|      |     |           |       |      |
|      |     |           |       |      |
|      |     |           |       |      |

## Today's Plans:

_____
_____

## Cruise Day #_____
## Date: ___/___/___

## Places:

## Weather:

## Activities List:

_____
_____
_____
_____
_____
_____

## My favorite foods & drinks:

_____
_____
_____
_____
_____
_____
_____
_____
_____
_____

## My best experience today:

_____
_____
_____
_____
_____
_____
_____
_____
_____

_____
_____
_____
_____
_____
_____
_____
_____
_____
_____
_____
_____
_____
_____
_____
_____
_____
_____
_____
_____
_____
_____
_____
_____

# Notes & Memories

# Photos & Memorabilia

## Photos & Memorabilia

**Today's Plans:**

_____
_____
_____

**Cruise Day #_____**
**Date: ____/____/____**

**Places:**

**Weather:**

**Activities List:**

_____
_____
_____
_____
_____
_____

**My favorite foods & drinks:**

_____
_____
_____
_____
_____
_____
_____
_____
_____
_____
_____

**My best experience today:**

_____
_____
_____
_____
_____
_____
_____
_____
_____
_____
_____

## Notes & Memories

# Notes &
# Memories

# Photos & Memorabilia

# Photos & Memorabilia

## Today's Plans:

_____

_____

_____

### Cruise Day #_____
### Date: ___/___/___

## Places:

## Weather:

## Activities List:

_____

_____

_____

_____

_____

_____

## My favorite foods & drinks:

## My best experience today:

## Notes & Memories

# Notes & Memories

# Photos & Memorabilia

# Photos & Memorabilia

## Today's Plans:

_____
_____

## Cruise Day #_____
## Date: ___ / ___ / ___

### Places:
🌐🏦🧭🪧

### Weather:
☀️ 🌧️ ❄️ 🌡️

### Activities List: 📍🏨📷🗺️
_____
_____
_____
_____
_____

## My favorite foods & drinks:

_____
_____
_____
_____
_____
_____
_____
_____
_____
_____

## My best experience today:

_____
_____
_____
_____
_____
_____
_____
_____
_____
_____
_____

## Notes & Memories

# Notes & Memories

# Photos & Memorabilia

## Photos & Memorabilia

**Today's Plans:**
_____
_____
_____

**Cruise Day #_____**
**Date: ___ / ___ / ___**

**Places:**

**Weather:**

**Activities List:**
_____
_____
_____
_____
_____
_____

**My favorite foods & drinks:**
_____
_____
_____
_____
_____
_____
_____
_____
_____
_____
_____
_____

**My best experience today:**
_____
_____
_____
_____
_____
_____
_____
_____
_____
_____
_____
_____

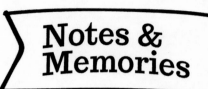

# Notes & Memories

## Photos & Memorabilia

# Photos & Memorabilia

## Today's Plans:

_____
_____
_____

**Cruise Day #_____**
**Date: ___/___/___**

### Places:

🌐 🏛 🧭 🪧

### Weather:

☀️ 🌧 ❄️ 🌡

### Activities List:

📍 🏢 📷 🗺

_____
_____
_____
_____
_____

## My favorite foods & drinks:

_____
_____
_____
_____
_____
_____
_____
_____
_____

## My best experience today:

_____
_____
_____
_____
_____
_____
_____
_____
_____

# Notes & Memories

# Photos & Memorabilia

# Photos & Memorabilia

# Today's Plans:

_____

_____

Cruise Day #_____
Date: ____/____/____

## Places:

## Weather:

## Activities List:

_____

_____

_____

_____

_____

_____

## My favorite foods & drinks:

## My best experience today:

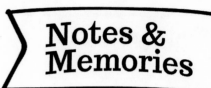

Notes &
Memories

# Notes & Memories

# Photos & Memorabilia

# Photos & Memorabilia

**Today's Plans:**

_____
_____
_____

**Cruise Day #_____**
**Date: ____ / ____ / ____**

**Places:**

**Weather:**

**Activities List:**

_____
_____
_____
_____
_____
_____

**My favorite foods & drinks:**

**My best experience today:**

# Notes & Memories

# Photos & Memorabilia

## Photos & Memorabilia

**Today's Plans:**

_____

_____

_____

**Cruise Day  #_____**
**Date: ___ / ___ / ___**

**Places:**

**Weather:**

**Activities List:**

_____

_____

_____

_____

_____

_____

**My favorite foods & drinks:**

**My best experience today:**

# Notes & Memories

# Photos & Memorabilia

# Photos & Memorabilia

## Today's Plans:

_____
_____

**Cruise Day #_____**
**Date: ___/___/___**

### Places:

### Weather:

### Activities List:

_____
_____
_____
_____
_____
_____

## My favorite foods & drinks:

## My best experience today:

# Notes & Memories

# Photos & Memorabilia

# Photos & Memorabilia

**Today's Plans:**

_____
_____
_____

**Cruise Day #_____**
**Date: ___/___/___**

**Places:**

**Weather:**

**Activities List:**

_____
_____
_____
_____
_____
_____

**My favorite foods & drinks:**

_____
_____
_____
_____
_____
_____
_____
_____
_____
_____

**My best experience today:**

_____
_____
_____
_____
_____
_____
_____
_____
_____
_____

# Notes & Memories

# Photos & Memorabilia

# Photos & Memorabilia

**Today's Plans:**

_____
_____

**Cruise Day #_____**
**Date: ___/___/___**

**Places:**

🌐🏯🧭🪧

**Weather:**

☀️🌧️❄️🌡️

**Activities List:**  📍🏢📷🗺️

_____
_____
_____
_____
_____
_____

**My favorite foods & drinks:**

_____
_____
_____
_____
_____
_____
_____
_____
_____
_____
_____
_____
_____

**My best experience today:**

_____
_____
_____
_____
_____
_____
_____
_____
_____
_____
_____
_____
_____

# Notes & Memories

# Photos & Memorabilia

# Photos & Memorabilia

**Today's Plans:**

_____
_____

**Cruise Day #_____**
**Date: ___/___/___**

**Places:**

**Weather:**

**Activities List:**

_____
_____
_____
_____
_____
_____

**My favorite foods & drinks:**

_____
_____
_____
_____
_____
_____
_____
_____
_____

**My best experience today:**

_____
_____
_____
_____
_____
_____
_____
_____
_____

# Notes & Memories

# Photos & Memorabilia

# Photos & Memorabilia

**Today's Plans:**

_____
_____

**Cruise Day #_____**
**Date: ___ / ___ / ___**

**Places:**

**Weather:**

**Activities List:**
_____
_____
_____
_____
_____
_____

**My favorite foods & drinks:**

**My best experience today:**

# Notes & Memories

# Photos & Memorabilia

# Photos & Memorabilia

**Today's Plans:**

_____
_____

**Cruise Day #_____**
**Date: ___/___/___**

**Places:**

**Weather:**

**Activities List:**

_____
_____
_____
_____
_____

**My favorite foods & drinks:**

_____
_____
_____
_____
_____
_____
_____
_____
_____
_____

**My best experience today:**

_____
_____
_____
_____
_____
_____
_____
_____
_____
_____

# Notes & Memories

# Photos & Memorabilia

# Photos & Memorabilia

**Today's Plans:**

_____
_____
_____

**Cruise Day #_____**
**Date: ___/___/___**

**Places:**

**Weather:**

**Activities List:**
_____
_____
_____
_____
_____
_____

**My favorite foods & drinks:**

_____
_____
_____
_____
_____
_____
_____
_____
_____
_____

**My best experience today:**

_____
_____
_____
_____
_____
_____
_____
_____
_____
_____

# Notes & Memories

# Photos & Memorabilia

# Photos & Memorabilia

## Today's Plans:

_____

_____

## Cruise Day #_____
## Date: ___/___/___

### Places:

### Weather:

### Activities List:

_____

_____

_____

_____

_____

_____

## My favorite foods & drinks:

_____

_____

_____

_____

_____

_____

_____

_____

_____

_____

_____

_____

## My best experience today:

_____

_____

_____

_____

_____

_____

_____

_____

_____

_____

_____

_____

# Notes & Memories

# Notes & Memories

# Photos & Memorabilia

# Photos & Memorabilia

**Today's Plans:**

_____
_____

**Cruise Day #_____**
**Date: ___/___/___**

**Places:**

**Weather:**

**Activities List:**
_____
_____
_____
_____
_____
_____

**My favorite foods & drinks:**

_____
_____
_____
_____
_____
_____
_____
_____
_____
_____
_____
_____
_____

**My best experience today:**

_____
_____
_____
_____
_____
_____
_____
_____
_____
_____
_____
_____
_____

## Notes & Memories

# Notes & Memories

# Photos & Memorabilia

# Photos & Memorabilia

Made in United States
North Haven, CT
13 June 2023

37693912R00069